This book is to be
the las

STARTERS

Pets

Liz Gogerly

W

an imprint of Hodder Children's Books

Language consultant: Andrew Burrell
Design: Perry Tate Design
Picture research: Glass Onion Pictures

Published in Great Britain in 2004
by Hodder Wayland, an imprint of
Hodder Children's Books

The publishers would like to thank the following for allowing us to reproduce their
pictures in this book: Angela Hampton / Family Life Picture Library; 6, 7, 10, 15
(top), 16, 17 (top), 19 (bottom), 20, 22 (bottom) / Getty Images; title page, contents
page, 8 (top), 9 (bottom), 12, 13, 15 (bottom), 17 (bottom), 18, 19 (top),
21 (bottom), 23 / Hodder Wayland Picture Library; 4, 8 (bottom), 11, 21 (top) /
Corbis; cover, 5, 9 (top), 14, 22 (top)

A catalogue record for this book is available from the British Library.

ISBN: 0750245530

Printed and bound in Singapore

Hodder Children's Books
A division of Hodder Headline Limited
338 Euston Road, London NW1 3BH

Subject consultant: Elaine Pendlebury, PDSA Senior Veterinary Surgeon

PDSA is Britain's leading veterinary charity. Visit their web site www.pdsa.org.uk for
useful information about looking after your pet. To join the PDSA Pet Protectors club
for young animal lovers e-mail petprotectors@pdsa.org.uk or phone 01952 290999.

Contents

Our best friends

Pets are often called our best friends.
A pet might be soft and furry
and lovely to cuddle.

Some cats like to be
stroked. It makes
them purr.

It might be strange and creeeepy and interesting to watch.

It could be big and bouncy, and very noisy. **WOOF! WOOF!**

A dog is fun to play with.

Some people have
pets that become
more than just a
best friend. They
help them to live
their lives.

Guide dogs for
the blind help
people by being
their eyes.

Pets are good company if a person lives on their own. Many people talk to their animals.

Walking the dog is a good way to get out of the house and make new friends.

A new baby

When you get a new
pet it's very exciting.
Many people choose
a baby animal.

This puppy is old
enough to leave
its mother. The girl
has chosen it to
be her pet.

8

A new pet might feel strange and shy. If you are very gentle then it will soon feel at home.

Some pets need to be kept together so that they don't feel lonely.

Guinea pigs like to live together.

A place to sleep

Pets need a place where they feel safe.
And a snug bed where they can sleep.

This puppy
has a cosy
basket with a
warm blanket
to snuggle into.

These guinea pigs
have plenty of fresh
sawdust to lie on in
their hutch.

Fish don't need warm beds but they must have a clean bowl or tank. Clean water makes it easy for them to breathe.

A bite to eat

Baby animals love to eat. Just like you and me they need a good diet to help them **GROW**.

A foal might enjoy some tasty pellets. They contain lots of vitamins.

Baby rabbits enjoy eating **crunchy** carrots.

Puppies chew on anything – shoes, bags, hats and even smelly socks! But to help them grow they need special puppy food.

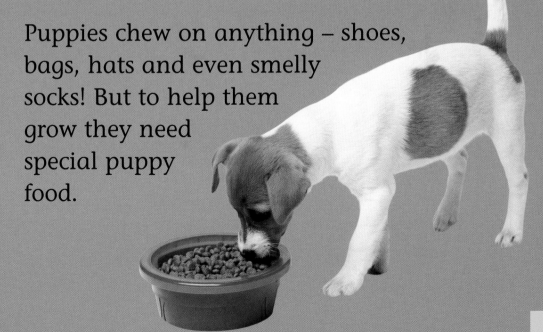

Lessons in life

As a pet grows up it learns new things – just like we do.

Some animals need to learn how to trust you. This takes time and patience.

A young pony might learn to wear a harness. It also learns to like being brushed.

A new pet soon learns where it can go to the toilet.

This kitten is using a litter tray.

Young animals quickly find out who their friends are too.

Pets like to play too!

Not all animals like to play together but they love to play with us.

Playing games is good exercise for all animals.

A hamster might enjoy rolling about in an exercise ball. Be careful it doesn't get tired though.

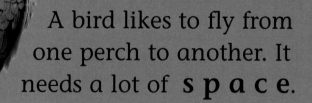

A bird likes to fly from one perch to another. It needs a lot of **s p a c e**.

As long as an animal has lots to see and do it is unlikely to get bored.

Wild at heart

Some of the things that pets do remind us that all animals once lived in the wild.

Hamsters store up food in their cheek pouches.

Some dogs dig holes and bury their bones in the garden.

A rabbit might stamp it's back foot on the ground to warn of danger.

Sometimes cats sharpen their claws on furniture or trees.

19

Poorly pets

From time to time our pets can get sick. They might need to go to the vet.

Some pets find this frightening. They shiver and shake in the waiting room.

The vet will give your pet
a check-up. They might give
it some medicine or an
injection to help make
it better.

And you can help your pet by letting it get
the peace and quiet it needs
to get better.

Making babies

One day our pets
become old
enough to make
babies of
their own.

If you have a male
and female animal
and keep them
together, then
they'll probably
have babies.

Watch out, often there are lots of babies!

They might be soft and furry, **big** and b⁰uₙcy, or even strange and c r e e p y. But most importantly, like all pets, the babies need a caring home.

Glossary and index

Diet A pet's diet is the food that it eats every day. **12**

Foal A baby horse. **12**

Guide dog A dog that has been specially trained to help blind people. **6**

Harness Straps that go over a horse's head to control it. **14**

Injection Medicine that is put into the body using a needle and syringe. **21**

Medicine A type of liquid or tablet that you take when you are ill to make you feel better. **21**

Perch A rod or branch that a bird can sit on. **17**

Vet A veterinary surgeon. A person who has been trained to look after sick animals. **20, 21**

Wild An animal that is not looked after by people. **18**